Jammin' Janet's First 100+ Rock Beats for Drumset

(a Slammin' Simon publication)

check out all the guides at
JamminJanet.com *or* **SlamminSimon.com**

Jammin' Janet plays . . .

prologix
practice pads

VIC FIRTH
drumsticks

and supports the . . .

HIT LIKE A GIRL

contest

Hi! My name is Janet. Welcome to my book,
First 100+ Rock Beats for Drumset.
You can call me Jammin' Janet like everyone
else does. I got that nickname because
I'm always jamming out on my drums –
my all-time favorite thing to do!

This is my pet and #1 BFF, Viva.
That's short for Vivace or Vivacissimo,
which are fancy music words that mean
lively and fast. Don't let her being a
snail fool you; she gets going pretty
quickly when she wants to.
She will, however, be the
first to tell you that the
key to drumming super
fast is actually practicing
super slowly. She reminds me
all the time . . . and she's right.
More on that later.
For now, I want to get
you started rocking out ASAP!
Grab your favorite drumsticks,
get to your drumset and let's get to it.

This part of the set is called the hi-hat and has two hi-hat cymbals that can be opened and closed using the hi-hat stand that they're mounted on.

For now, keep the hi-hat closed, which will probably mean keeping your left foot held down on the pedal to hold the cymbals tight together.

Next we're going to do some counting.
Nice and loud, count: "1 & 2 & 3 & 4 &"

Then hit the closed hi-hat with your
right drumstick with every count.

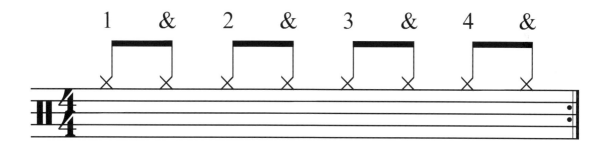

You just played what are called 8th notes. They get
that name because, in a regular measure (or bar) of
music, 8 of them fit inside. Look up above there again.
See? You played 8 of them!

Play that measure again but, this time, don't stop
at the end of it. The two dots and two lines at the
end are called a repeat sign, telling us to go back
and do the measure again. No taking a break at
the end . . . zip back to the beginning and keep your
counting and playing going another time through.
Or maybe a whole bunch of times through!

Got that? Good.

The big drum on the floor (with another pedal
connected to it) is the bass drum. It's usually the
largest piece of the drumset and usually has
the lowest pitch.

Put your right foot on the bass drum pedal and,
moving from your ankle, give it a few solid thumps.
Pretty cool, right?

Now let's add a couple bass drum notes in with
the 8th notes we were playing on the hi-hat.
Count this one (out loud) and play the hi-hat the
same way but, when you say 1 and 3, hit both the
hi-hat and the bass drum at exactly the same time.

Viva just leaned in and said to tell you that,
if the two don't line up perfectly together, just slow
the whole exercise down. Once you get it down
at a slow speed (or tempo), you can then gradually
speed it up to faster tempos.

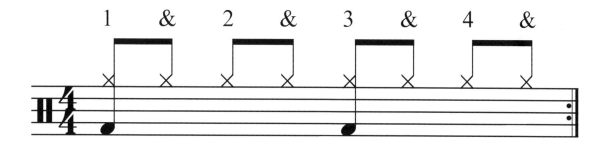

Repeat this over and over until it's comfortable.

One more drum to learn about for now: the snare drum. Sitting right in front of you, the snare has metal strands (called snare wires) underneath that push against the bottom drumhead and give the drum a snappy, metallic sound.

Time to add it to our exercise. Here the hi-hat and bass drum stay the same as before but, every time you count 2 and 4, hit both the hi-hat and snare drum at the same time. Start slowly and make sure each limb plays exactly when it's supposed to.

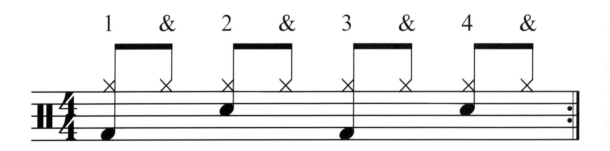

Um, that is amazing and, you know what? You're now playing the most popular rock beat of all time. That's right, rockstar, you are officially a rock drummer! Tell your parents; tell your friends; it's world tour time for you!

Well, okay . . . maybe not just yet. I guess there are some other things we still need to learn before we hit the big stage with all the bright lights and screaming fans.

I was serious, though, about the fact that you just played the most popular rock beat of all time. But let's learn some others. For now, keep counting, keep those 8th notes going on the hi-hat, keep the snare drum on 2 and 4, and let's explore some bass drum variations.

The first one has us adding extra bass drum notes on the "& of 1" and the "& of 3." Putting the hi- hat and bass together two times in a row can sometimes be tricky, so take your time on this one.

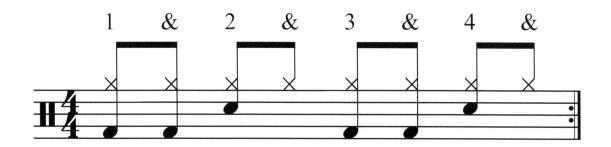

Here are a bunch more for you to work through.
Have fun and I'll see you on the other side!

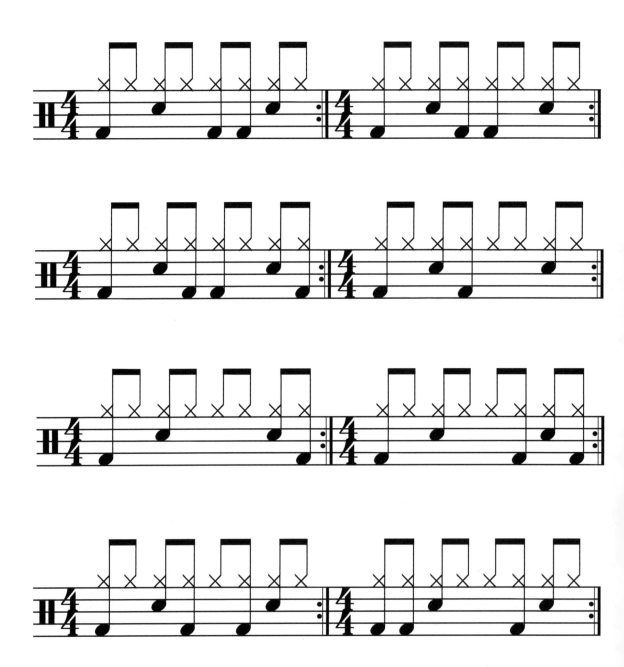

Nice work, you! There are lots and lots of 8th-note beats that we can play – these are really only a sample of what's possible. But it seems like you have a good handle on these, and there are so many other types of beats that we want to show you, so let's do something a tiny bit different!

For this next section, we're still going to COUNT 8th notes but we'll sometimes be PLAYING something called quarter notes. Two 8th notes fit into the same space as one quarter note, meaning that quarter notes are played half as fast as 8ths. If that seems confusing right now (I know it did at first to me), don't worry. It will make way more sense once we get playing them!

For starters, let's count 8th notes again but we'll only hit the hi-hat on every other count – the numbers only. Don't hit the hi-hat when you say "&."

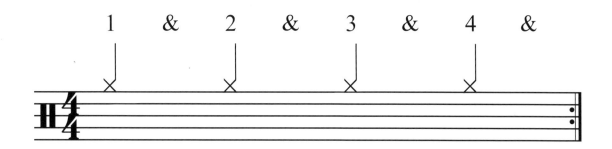

When you've got that,
add bass drum on beats 1 and 3 . . .

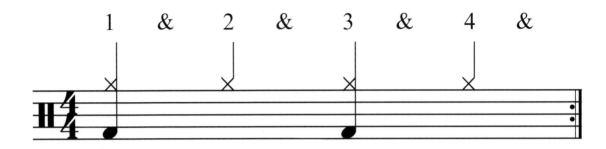

. . . and then snare drum on 2 and 4.
Remember, no playing on the "&"s.

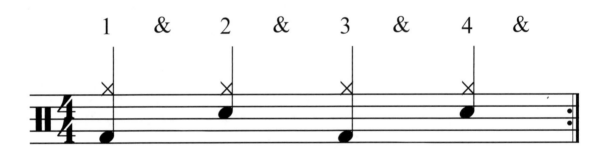

There you go! Notice anything similar about the bass
drum and snare drum pattern? This is the quarter-note
version of our first complete 8th-note rock beat
(on page 8). The hi-hat part changed but the bass
and snare are exactly the same! Sometimes that
original 8th-note beat might be perfect for a song.
Other times, it might be cool to use this new
quarter-note one instead.

Okay, this one is going to use all of those
same notes that we just played . . .
plus more bass drum notes on the
"& of 1" and the "& of 3."

The hardest part of this one is letting your bass
drum play those extra notes but NOT letting
your hi-hat add them in, too.

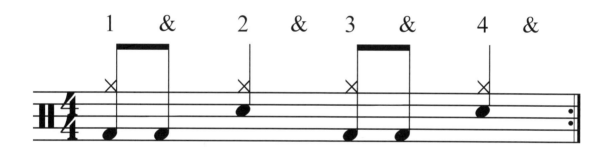

As always, if that's a bit tricky,
go slower and slower until you find
a speed that you can play it perfectly at.

Once you've got the hang of that, keeping rockin'
through all the rest of these quarter-note beats.

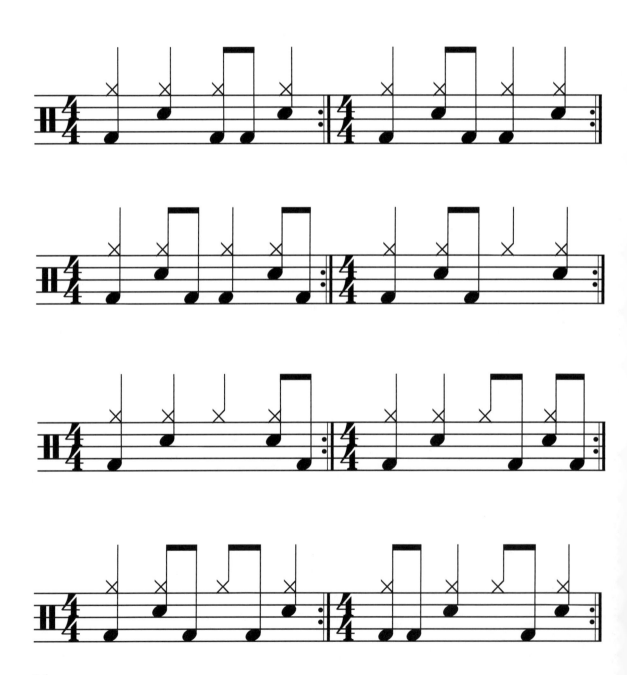

We learned that quarter notes are half as fast as 8th notes. Now we get to go the opposite direction and play 16th notes, which are twice as fast as 8ths! Since we have to fit even more notes in (exactly 16 in every measure), we also have to make a tiny change to our counting.

By the way, you HAVE still been counting out loud, haven't you?? Good.

We will still be counting our 8th notes ("1 & 2 & 3 & 4 &") but are now adding an "E" right after every number and an "A" (usually sounds like "ah") right after every "&." That turns our new 16th-note counting into "1 E & A 2 E & A 3 E & A 4 E & A"

Take your time and just practice counting out loud like that for a while. It can be a real tongue twister! But like everything, you'll master it with a little practice.

Got it? Suhweet! Let's play some 16th-note beats.

Start again with only the hi-hat. Count your 16ths
and play a hi-hat note on every single one.

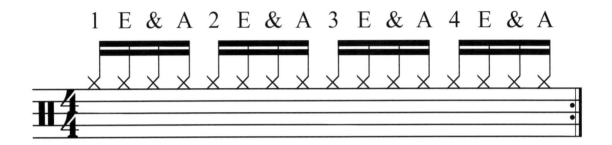

I bet you know what's next.
Add bass drum on beats 1 and 3 . . .

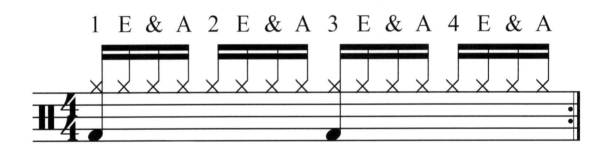

. . . and snare drum on 2 and 4.

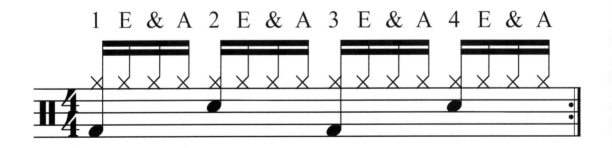

There you have it, your first 16th-note rock beat! These are used in lots of musical styles, like funk and R&B.

Like we did earlier with our 8th-note beats, let's add extra bass drum notes on the "& of 1" and the "& of 3." One warning here: don't play the bass drum with any of the "E" or "A" counts. Not yet anyway, but we will do that right after this.

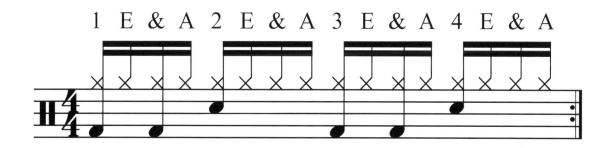

Up for a tough one? As promised, it's "E" and "A" time. Let's play bass drum on the "E of 1" and the "A of 2."

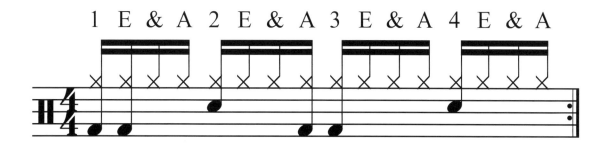

There are so many fun possibilities. I'll give you a bunch more to tackle but, first, Viva wants to remind you of a few things . . .

Viva's Reminders

Okay, let's get to it!
Here are a bunch more 16th-note beats.

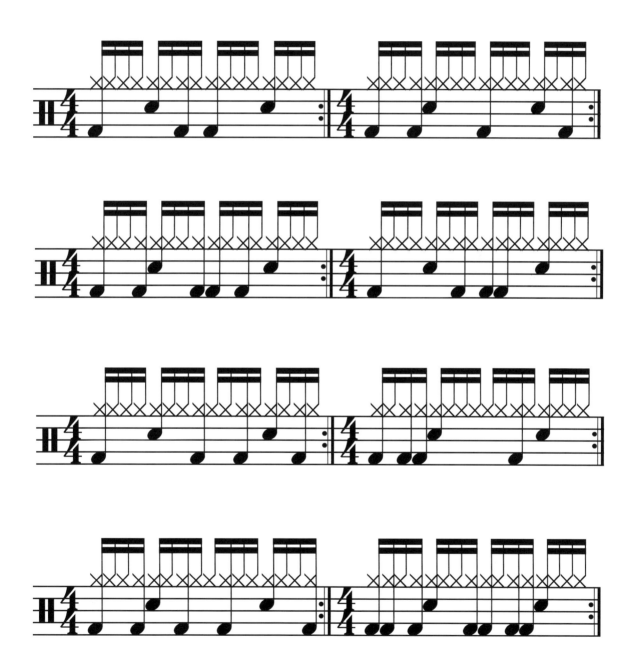

Now hold up a second. Those 16th-note beats were pretty cool, but how would you like to learn how to play them even faster? I thought so, and I can't wait to show you how! We're going to play some of the same grooves again but with a couple of important changes.

First, instead of our right hand playing all of the hi-hat notes, we're going to alternate back and forth between our right and left hands, playing a Right-Left-Right-Left (or R L R L) sticking pattern all the way through the measure.

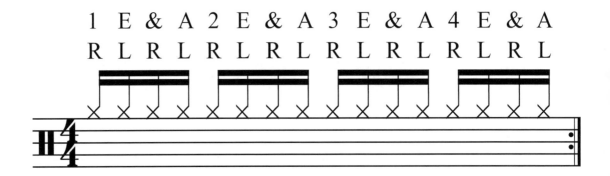

Next we'll add bass drum on beats 1 and 3.

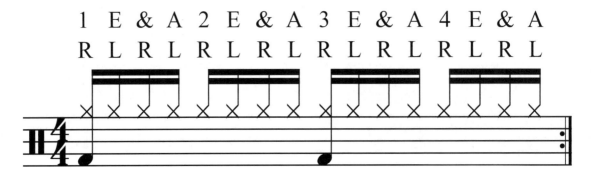

Then, at the beginning of beats 2 and 4, our right
hand travels over and hits the snare drum but then
races back to the hi-hat so that the hands can
keep alternating over there.

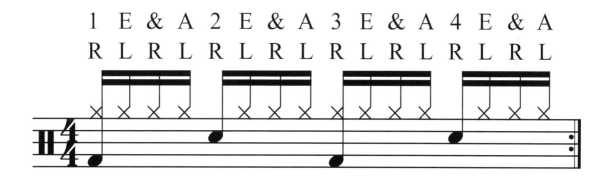

Nice! Now add bass drum again on the "& of 1" and
"& of 3." Make sure that every bass drum note is played
exactly when your right stick plays the hi-hat.

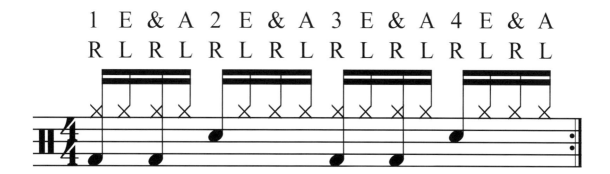

Now let's practice the bass drum playing
at the same time as the left stick on the hi-hat.
Here we'll add bass on the "A of 1" and the
"E of 3." The bass drum lines up with the right
hand on beats 1 and 3, but then with the left hand
on both of our added notes.

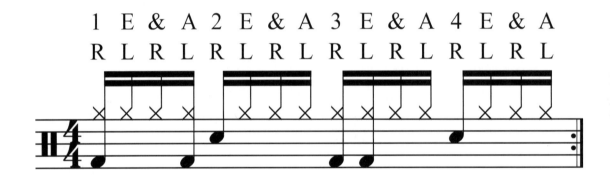

Go very slowly and you will eventually
get the hang of these. Once you do, then continue
on to all of the fun beats on the next page.

Remember to keep counting and to keep alternating from hand to hand (R L R L). Be sure that every bass drum note on an "E" or "A" lands at the same time as your left stick plays the hi-hat.

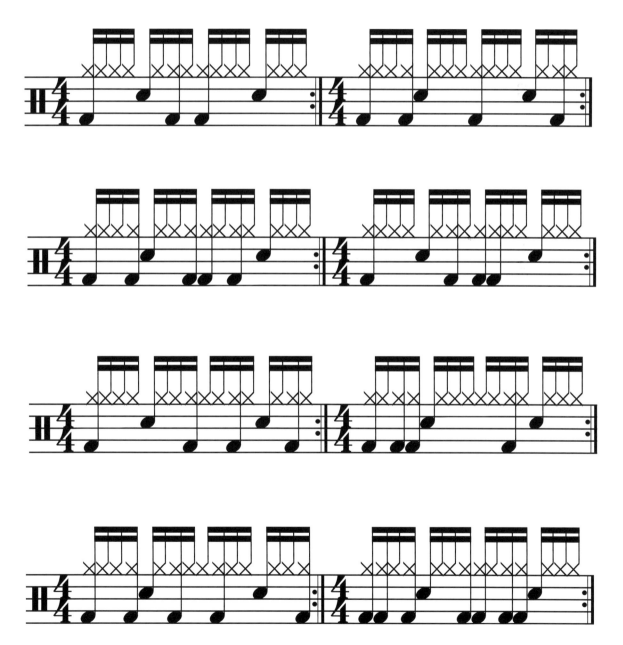

You've played 8th notes. You've played 16th notes. Now let's mix them up and get downright funky!

Even though we won't always be PLAYING 16th notes on the following beats, it will be very helpful if we are always COUNTING 16th notes. It will help us keep all the notes in the right places. I think you'll see what I mean as we get into it.

Our first short exercise is going to be made up of just one 8th note + two 16th notes. Hi-hat and bass drum play perfectly together on the 8th note, and then play separately on the two 16th notes (hi-hat alone on the "&" and bass alone on the "A").

Even though you're not actually hitting anything when you count the "E" . . . DO KEEP COUNTING IT! It will help you leave the precise amount of space between the hi-hat notes.

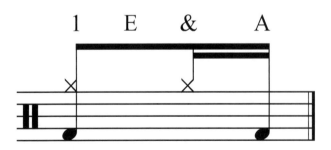

The next exercise is the same but using snare drum instead of bass drum. Hi-hat and snare drum play together on the 8th note, and then separately on the two 16th notes (hi-hat on the "&" and snare on the "A").

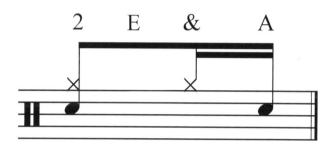

I'm sure you already know what's next:
yep, putting both of those exercises together.

Keep counting those 16th notes out loud,
all the way through!

Instead of adding bass and snare notes on the
"A" counts, let's add some on the "E" counts.

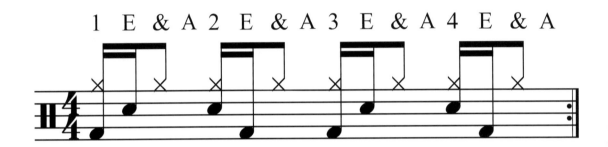

And combine both of those ideas—
"E" and "A" notes all over the place!

But still make sure to only play hi-hat on the "&" counts.

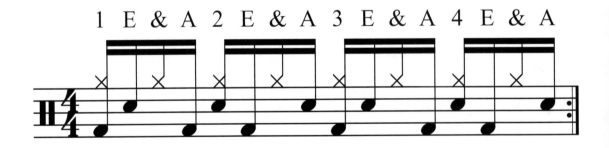

Again, there are so many variations of this idea that
we could play. Here are some of my favorites!

Okay, now we get to explore some of Viva's favorites!

Up until here, we've been playing snare drum on beats 2 and 4. When playing with a Double-Time Feel, we're going to play snare drum on the "&" of each beat, which will eventually make these feel like they are twice as fast (or double time) compared to our earlier grooves.

You'll find uses for this feel in all kinds of musical styles. From country to punk to polka and more, it's a handy one to have in your back pocket.

To start getting a handle on this feel, let's play hi-hat on every 8th note, bass drum on 1, 2, 3 and 4, and snare drum on all of the "&"s.

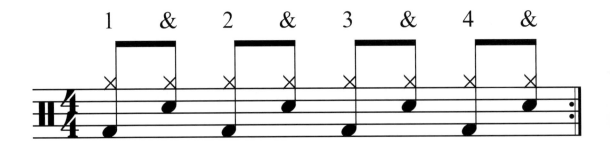

Hear how different that sounds from our other patterns? Cool, for sure, but it's all about to get even cooler.

We played bass and snare on some "E"s and "A"s on our Funky Beats and we can do the same with these. First off, let's play two bass drums at the end of our groove – one lands right on beat 4 and the other right after it, on the "E of 4." Make sure that playing those two 16th notes with your bass drum doesn't mess up your hi-hat, still chugging away with straight, steady 8th notes. And keep that snare drum solid on the "& of 4."

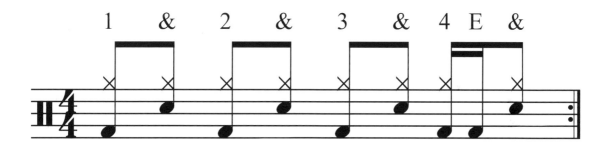

This time, add an extra bass drum on the "A of 2" instead, spacing it out perfectly between the snare and bass that surround it.

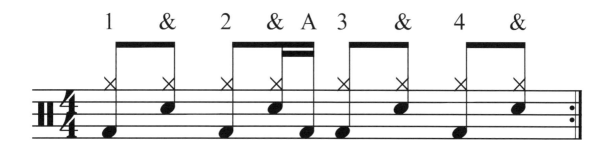

Seems like you're getting the hang of this, so go ahead and combine both of our last two exercises into one. Viva says to remind you that, even though these will sound super fast and rockin' once you get them going, you should start out nice and slow. Also, your bass drum foot is playing quite a few notes, so be sure to stay as relaxed as possible. That will help you play these even faster later on.

Let's make that beat even funkier. Shift the bass drum that has been on beat 2 one 16th later (to the "E of 2") and shift the bass drum that has been on beat 4 one 16th earlier (to the "A of 3").

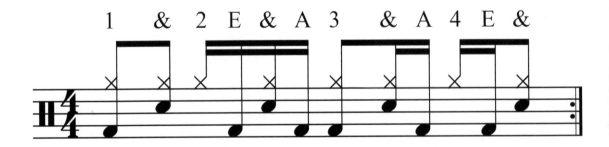

Now that's some funky stuff! The sound of beats like this makes Viva bob her head with the groove.

Here are a bunch more beats in this double-time feel.
As a bonus, we tossed in a few that have extra snare
and/or hi-hat notes dropped in, too, so watch out for those.

Take your time . . . it will be worth it!

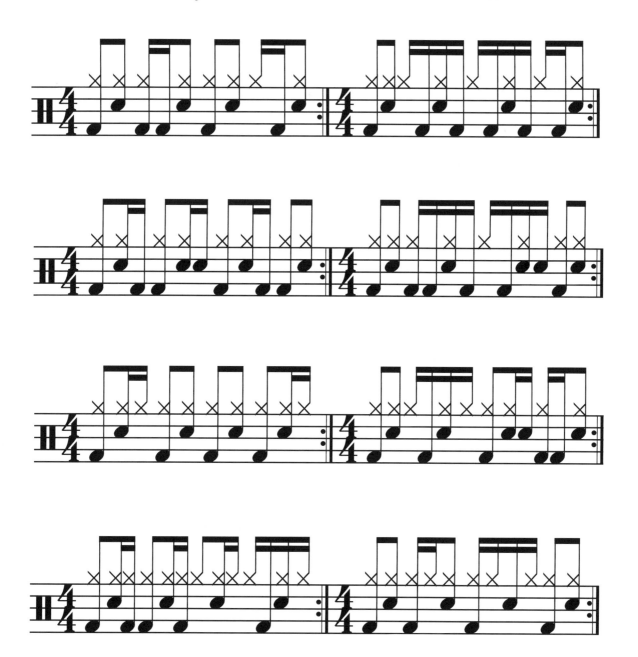

This next feel is sort of opposite of those double-time beats, at least that's the case with the snare drum rhythm. Instead of playing snare on all of the "&"s, we'll be playing it on all of the downbeats (the very first note of beats 1, 2, 3 and 4).

Hundreds of classic, hit songs that came out of the city of Detroit, Michigan many years ago featured this drumset beat. Detroit's nickname was "Motor City" and the style of music coming from there at the time became known as Motown. Not all Motown songs use this beat – and it definitely pops up in other styles, as well (punk again comes to mind) – but it's used on so many of my personal favorite Motown tunes that Viva and I often call it The Motown Beat.

The key is keeping the snare drum on all of the downbeats and, here, we'll do the same with the bass drum.

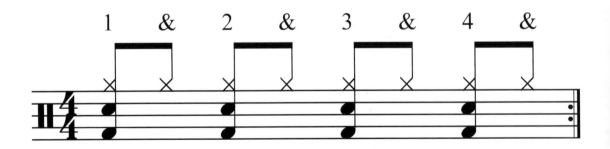

Now let's move the bass drum to the "&" of every beat. This creates something completely backward from our first double time groove.

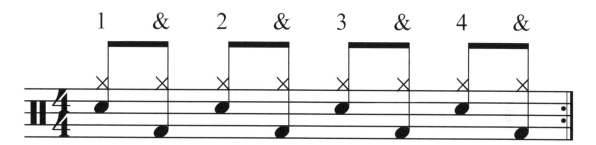

How about bass on some downbeats and on some "&"s?

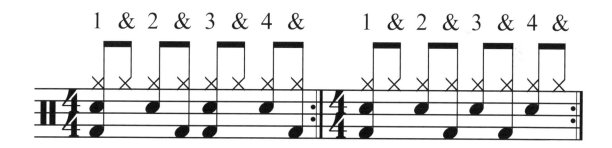

And maybe on an "A" here and there?
I think you're getting the hang of this.

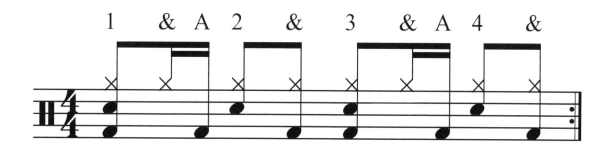

Have fun working through the rest of these
variations. Don't forget to keep it slow at first . . .
and count, count, count.

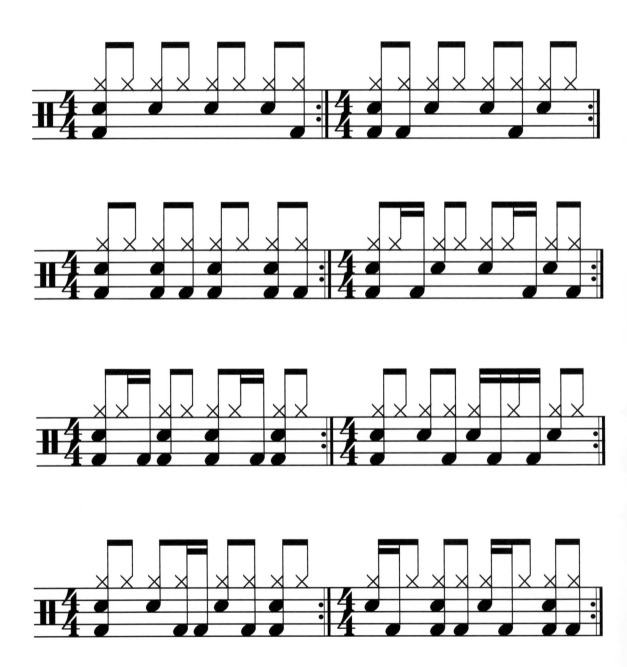

Our Double-Time beats had us playing grooves that felt twice as fast as our original patterns. Now it's time to go the other direction and play some Half-Time beats. As you might have already guessed by their name, these sound like they are HALF as fast as our regular patterns. Instead of snare drum falling on beats 2 and 4 of each measure, it will just land on beat 3.

This is a cool, laid-back feel that can played all the way through some songs . . . but I love it most when it's snuck into the middle of a straight-ahead rock tune. That way, most of the song has a standard rock feel, with the snare on 2 and 4, but then the whole band switches to a half-time feel (sometimes on a section of a song called the Bridge), making the music sound like it slowed way down. Coming out of that section, the band busts back into the original 2 and 4 feel and rocks out until the end. It's an awesome way to mix things up in the middle of a song!

Keeping your hi-hat 8th notes going, put bass drum on beat 1 and snare drum on beat 3.

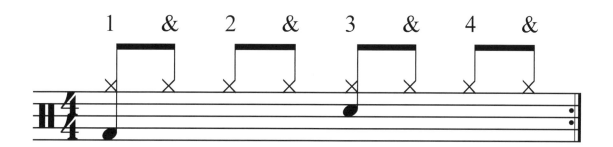

Are you able to hear how that pretty much sounds
like our first 16th-note groove, but twice as slow?
My drum teacher likes to say that it's
"exactly the same but completely different."
:)

We can add another bass drum on beat 2 . . .

. . . or on the "& of 2" . . .

. . . or on beat 4 . . .

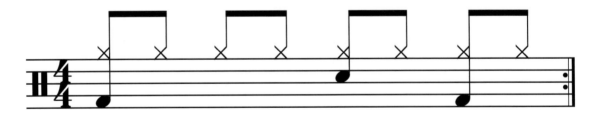

. . . or on all three of those spots!

Like so many other feels we've played, it's also possible to work in some bass drum 16th notes on some of the "E"s and "A"s. There are so many options; here are a number of them for you to try out.

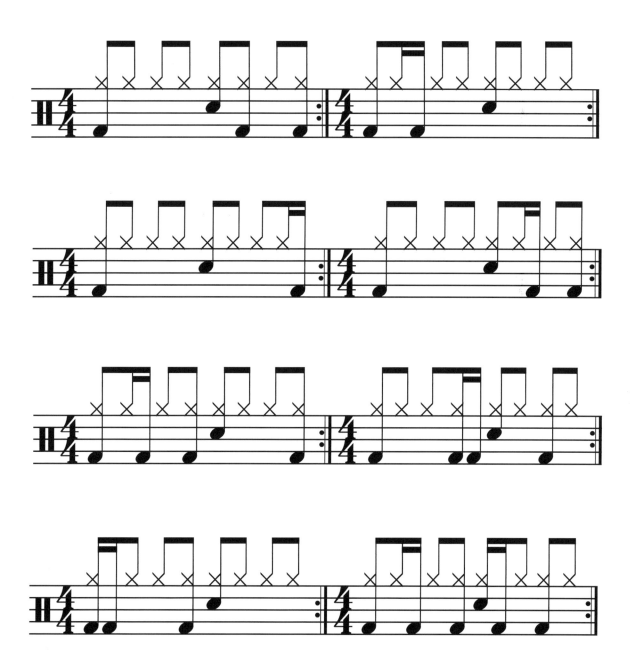

Every groove we've played so far in this book has used either 8th notes (groups of two) or 16th notes (groups of four) or a combination of 8ths and 16ths. These are even numbers and, in music, are what we call "duple" groupings. The last couple of feels we're going to look at are instead going to use groups of threes (or "triples"). When we are talking about counting and playing them in rhythms, musicians often call them "triplets."

Our triplets will look a lot like regular 8th notes, however there will be three of them beamed together in each beat and we'll see a bracket and number 3 over the top, as a constant reminder that we're playing 8th-note TRIPLETS instead of plain old 8th notes. That's important, because they're counted a little differently.

You may discover later that there are several ways to count triplets. We are going to keep it simple by still counting our beats ("1, 2, 3, 4") while inserting the two-syllable word "trip-let" after each number. As always, keep your counting steady, with all counts being the same speed and evenly spaced.

"1 trip let 2 trip let 3 trip let 4 trip let"

Keep that counting going and play a hi-hat
on every single count.

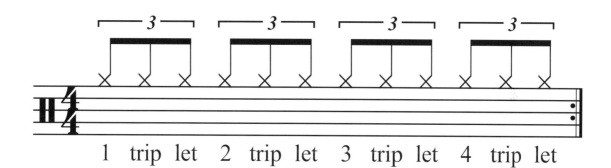

1　trip　let　2　trip　let　3　trip　let　4　trip　let

Like we have with so many of our other feels,
let's now add bass drum on beats 1 and 3,
and snare on beats 2 and 4.

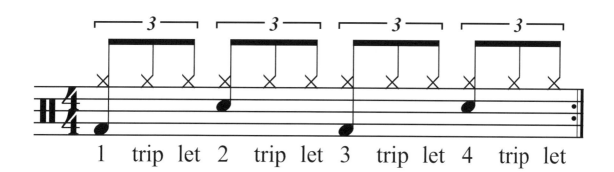

1　trip　let　2　trip　let　3　trip　let　4　trip　let

Viva said that I should take a second to point out that, even though we've written this one here in 4/4 time signature (meaning that there are 4 quarter notes per measure), there's another time signature that you'll often find this groove written in: 12/8. That means that there are twelve 8th notes per measure.

In 12/8 time, instead of counting "1 trip let 2 trip let 3 trip let 4 trip let," each 8th note gets its own beat and its own numbered count. Like this . . .

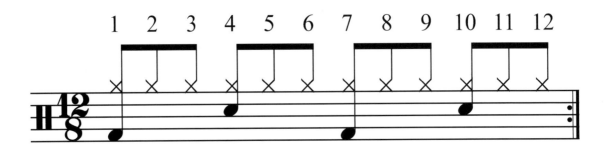

But sounds the same, right? For now, just be aware that you might see this written either way. Some people even count the 12/8 version as triplets just because they feel it's easier to say and count at faster speeds. Completely up to you! We'll write these as triplets, but I'm glad Viva reminded me to tell you about that.

This triplet or 12/8 feel is super useful if you ever jam with a Blues band, but you'll discover it used in lots of other styles, too. Let's play some more grooves like this!

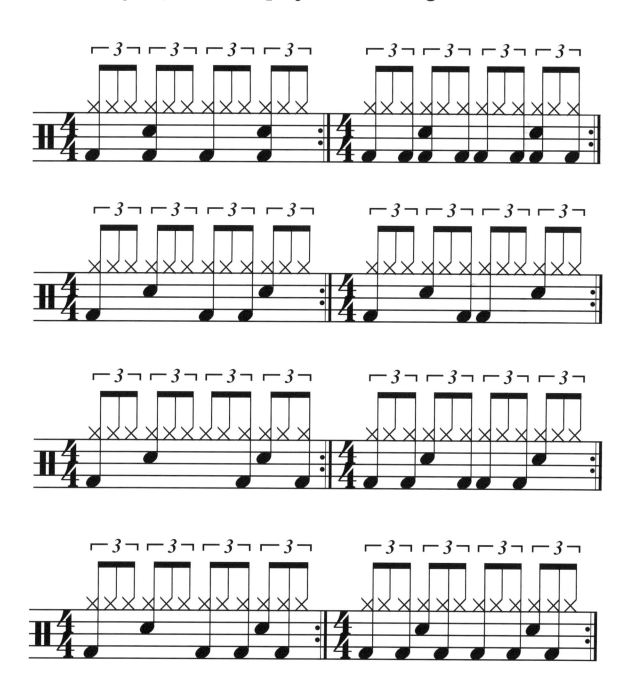

Wow, you've made it all the way here, to the last section of this book! Incredible job.

There are so many more music styles and drumset feels that we will explore in our other drum guides but there is one more that we HAVE to cover here before we say goodbye for now.

That feel is the Shuffle.

Since we recently learned how to play triplets, we'll base our shuffles here off of triplets, but there's also a 16th-note version that we'll probably check out at some other time.

Our triplet counting stays the same but we are actually NOT going to play the middle note of each triplet on the hi-hat. In place of the hi-hat note we've seen in that spot before, we now see an 8th-note rest, which looks like this . . .

$$\gamma$$

The 8th-note rest means that you are going to – that's right – REST instead of playing in that spot.

Make sure you keep your counting going steady even though some of the counts are on notes you actually play and some of the counts are in spots that you rest. Start off with only the hi-hat.

Oh, and Viva says to take your time.
:)

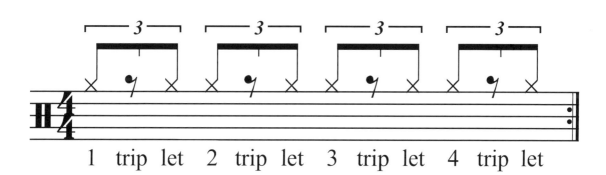

Of course, we have to add some bass and snare . . .

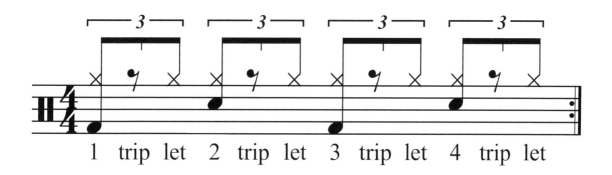

Voilà, you've got it! You're suddenly playing a shuffle, a fun little feel found in Rock, Blues, Jazz, and so much more.

How about a few more Shuffle beats?

There you have it . . .

8th-note and quarter-note beats;
16th-note beats (1-handed and 2-handed);
funky grooves; double-time and half-time feels;
Motown beats; triplets (or 12/8); and shuffles!

You've learned so many different drumset patterns.
At this point, you'll probably start recognizing
some of these beats in songs that you hear,
and you can also use them to start jamming
along with those songs.

Practice them a little bit every day and use your
creativity to make up your own grooves. Keep at
it and, before you know it, you'll be playing these
beats with your own rock band!

Viva and I want to give you a huge High 5 and
say thanks a million for hanging out and letting
us share all of these favorite grooves with you.
We hope to see again soon. Until then, take your
time, count out loud, and keep practicing!

Also, check out all my other guides at
JamminJanet.com to learn even more super
awesome drum rudiments, grooves, and fills.

Made in United States
Troutdale, OR
11/16/2024

24886379R00027